I thoroughly enjoyed and highly recommend to anyone who likes hilarious anecdotes, trashy narrative, and excellent soup Michael Congdon's "It is Best To Die In Your Sleep".

This collection of short stories and recipes, both laced with Southern Gothic, had me pissing myself with laughter. I love the book. Buy it.

>Eleanor Roth Atherton
>Orchestral musician, traveler & my little lover

He says these things just to embarrass me. I can barely show my face at Church. He's just doing this to upset me. I should never have listened to Dr. Spock. I feel awful. I wish I had never read this and I hope none of it is true.

>Louisa Congdon
>the author's mother

In a fantastic short story reminiscent of imagery created by Edgar Allen Poe, Michael Congdon skillfully weaves a visual snapshot of time between two individuals linked together using a beautiful mosaic of deteriorating bodies, aged surroundings, and an uncertain future. And then serves soup.

>Brent Heinze
>2nd runner up for Mr. Wet Platinum 1998

I've known Michael far longer than I really want to admit. It's so eye-opening to read about his experiences, see his flashes of humor, and get a good sense of where he's been and how he has become the amazing man he is today. I loved reading this book, and I can't wait to read the next one.

>Patricia Whipp
>embarrassed classmate 1983-1989

Michael and I have talked for ages. His conversations and writing are always great and descriptive – allowing me to easily "see" an event without having been there. Often encouraging me to laugh heartily.

>Sean Kline
>product manager, cat wrangler, resident skeptic

What a whore.

>Bryan Harrison
>the author's partner

Other Titles
S.O.U.P.S. (2005)
Miss Haverly & Miss Cavendish (2020)
Works in Progress
The Threshing Floor (A Book of Surrealist Prose)
Welcome to Piedmont, Virginia

It Is Best

to Die

in Your

Sleep

Credits
Edited by Larry J. Galante
Cover design by Aleksandar Milosavljevic
Cover art by Michael Congdon
Occasional interior artwork Ian Collin Redmond
Guest checks by Zack Johnson

It Is Best to Die in Your Sleep

MICHAEL CONGDON

To All My Hooligans

Copyright © 2020 Michael R. Congdon

All rights reserved. No part of this book may be reproduced or used in any manner without the prior written permission of the copyright owner, except for the use of brief quotations in a book review.

To request permissions, contact the publisher at
michael@om.nivorous.com

ISBN Paperback: 978-1-7357536-0-7

ISBN Ebook: 978-1-7357536-1-4

First paperback edition January 2020

This is a work of fiction. Names, characters, businesses, places, events, locales, and incidents are either the products of the author's imagination or used in a fictitious manner. Any resemblance to actual persons, living or dead, or actual events is purely coincidental.

Contents

Preface
International Mister Fancypants 2008 – I 1
Ergo Rex 9
Infelicitous and Ill-Judged 23
Gazpacho 37
Firing Employees 41
International Mister Fancypants 2008 – II 53
We Interrupt Your Regularly Scheduled Program – I 61
Mother's Day and the Blackening Banana 63
My Perfect Type 83
Gladys and Merl's Early Bird Special 87
Saag Panir 93
Tiramisu per la Famiglia 97
Tiramisu 102
Family Triptych – I 107
International Mister Fancypants 2008 – III 115
St. Petersburg (Not the One in Russia) 131
F**kin' Chestnuts 155
Cream of Chestnut Soup 161
International Mister Fancypants 2008 – IV 165
Café Septième 175
Pan Fried Polenta Triangles 178
We Interrupt Your Regularly Scheduled Program – II 183
A Sad, Sophomoric Assay 187
Diary of a Circuit Boy 191
Family Triptych – II 209
The French Quarter, Le Madeleine, and the Baths 217
Tomato Soup with Basil 228
On Being a New Resident of the French Quarter 231
The Five Year Push 247
International Mister Fancypants 2008 – V 249
Family Triptych – III 261
The Good, The Bad, and the Rawhide 267
Bubbles 273
Brazilian Black Bean Soup 283
International Mister Fancypants 2008 – VI 287

Mike Congdon
4/26/82

~~They~~ Then a little boy asked, "What's the matter?" The conductor said that one of the tracks on the bridge was very loose, and it may break when we ride over it. All of a sudden the lights went out, so we wouldn't know when we were going over the bridge.

My parent told me to sleep. Then they would try. I really tried because it was said that it was best to die in your sleep than anything else. We all slept.

The next thing heard was a loud bang then silence. Just before I died I saw our car filling up with water. Then black.